Classic Hymns for Violin and Piano

Advanced Solos
for the Church Violinist

Arranged by David Ritter

Piano Parts are located on a CD-ROM in the back of the book.

PUBLISHING COMPANY

lillenas.com

Contents

A Firm Foundation

includes

Standing on the Promises*
The Church's One Foundation**

Arranged by David Ritter

Majestically ♩ = ca. 116

"Standing on the Promises"

*Music by R. Kelso Carter.

**Music by Samuel S. Wesley.

Immortal, Invisible, God Only Wise

Music: Welsh Hymn Tune
Arranged by David Ritter

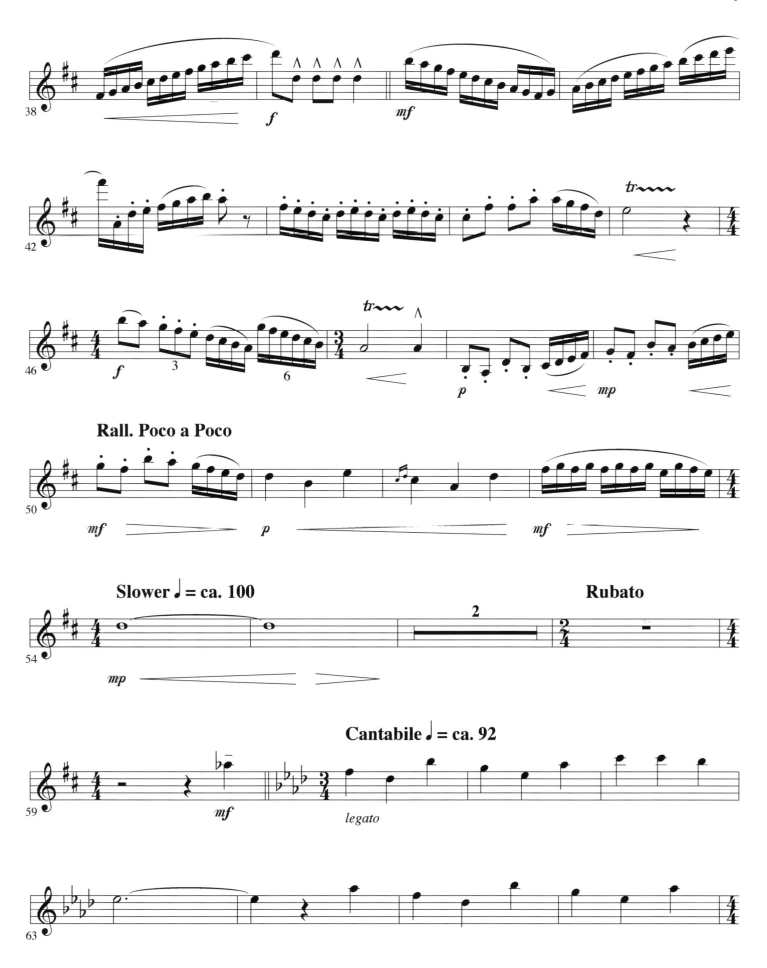

O God, Our Fortress

includes
A Mighty Fortress Is Our God*
Rock of Ages**
A Shelter in the Time of Storm***
O God, Our Help in Ages Past****

Arranged by David Ritter

*Music by Martin Luther.

**Music by Thomas Hastings.

***Music by Ira D. Sankey.

****Music by William Croft.

12

14

O God, Our Help in Ages Past

177093-14

Rejoice, the Lord Is King

Music by John Darwall
Arranged by David Ritter

16

Piu Mosso

Our Solid Rock
includes
The Solid Rock*
God Leads Us Along**
Where He Leads Me***

Arranged by David Ritter

*Music by William B. Bradbury.

**Music by G. A. Young.

***Music by John S. Norris.

18

Poco Rit. **Moderately** ♩ = ca. 85
"Where He Leads Me"

Poco Rit.

Rit. **Mysterioso** ♩ = ca. 80

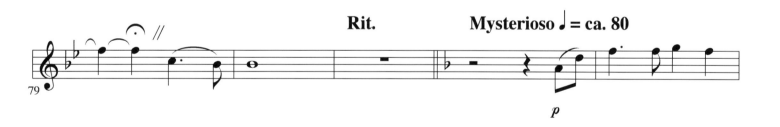

Accel.   **With Energy** ♩ = ca. 120

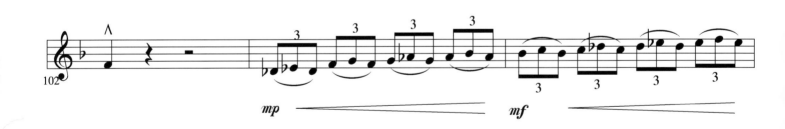

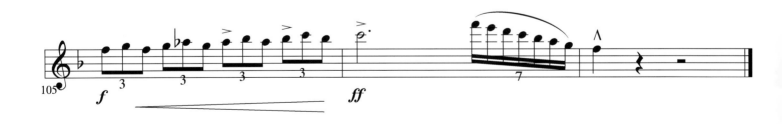

Our Great Savior

Music by Rowland H. Prichard
Arranged by David Ritter

Dedicated to My Daughter, Rachael Ritter Delgado

Sing!

includes

All Creatures of Our God and King*
Come, Christians, Join to Sing**
Joyful, Joyful, We Adore Thee***

Arranged by David Ritter

*Music: Geistliche Kirchengesange.

**Music: Traditional Spanish Melody.

***Music by Ludwig van Beethoven.

26

Christmas Night

includes
It Came upon the Midnight Clear*
The First Noel**

Arranged by David Ritter